Technology, Reading & Digital Literacy

Strategies to Engage the Reluctant Reader

L. Robert Furman

International Society for Technology in Education
EUGENE, OREGON • ARLINGTON, VA

Technology, Reading & Digital Literacy
Strategies to Engage the Reluctant Reader
L. Robert Furman

Editor: *Paul Wurster*
Associate Editor: *Emily Reed*
Production Manager: *Lynda Gansel*
Copy Editor: *Mike van Mantgem*
Proofreader: *Ann Skaugset*
Indexer: *Wendy Allex*
Book Interior Design and Production: *Kim McGovern*

Library of Congress Cataloging-in-Publication Data

Furman, L. Robert.
  Technology, reading, and digital literacy : strategies to engage
the reluctant reader / L. Robert Furman. — First edition.
    pages cm
  Includes index.
    ISBN 978-1-56484-358-6 (pbk.) — ISBN 978-1-56484-498-9
  (ebook)
    1. Computers and literacy. 2. Children—Books and reading.
  I. Title.
    LC149.5.F87 2015
    302.2'2440285—dc23

                                                        2014048984

First Edition
ISBN: 978-1-56484-358-6 (paperback)
ISBN: 978-1-56484-498-9 (ebook)

Printed in the United States of America

ISTE® is a registered trademark of the International Society
for Technology in Education.

About ISTE

The International Society for Technology in Education (ISTE) is the premier nonprofit organization serving educators and education leaders committed to empowering connected learners in a connected world. ISTE serves more than 100,000 education stakeholders throughout the world.

ISTE's innovative offerings include the ISTE Conference & Expo, one of the biggest, most comprehensive ed tech events in the world—as well as the widely adopted ISTE Standards for learning, teaching and leading in the digital age and a robust suite of professional learning resources, including webinars, online courses, consulting services for schools and districts, books, and peer-reviewed journals and publications. Visit iste.org to learn more.

Related ISTE Titles

Bookmapping: Lit Trips and Beyond
Terence W. Cavanaugh and Jerome Burg

Serious Comix: Engaging Students with Digital Storyboards
Eydie Wilson

To see all books available from ISTE, please visit iste.org/resources.

About the Author

 **L. Robert Furman** is principal at South Park Elementary Center in South Park, Pennsylvania, where he lives with his wife, Tiffeni, and two boys, Luke and Kyle. Prior to coming to South Park, Furman was an assistant middle school principal for Gateway School District in Monroeville, Pennsylvania.

Through the years, Furman has developed a keen interest in technology, and he constantly attempts to infuse instructional technology into school curriculum to enhance student learning. In 2011, he wrote *Instructional Technology Tools: A Professional Development Plan* and began speaking about the subject at state and national technology conferences. Furman blended his interests in technology and reading, and became passionate about supporting students with literature.

Furman began his teaching career as a music educator after graduating from West Virginia University in 1995. Music was his first love and remained an important part of his life as he continued his educational studies at Duquesne University in the Department of Supervision and Administration where he earned a doctorate in Educational Leadership.

Furman is a blogger for the *Huffington Post*, a writer for Scholastic's Reader Leader Forum, and a representative of Scholastic Books. He was recently honored as a national "20 to Watch" in educational technology by the National School Board Association, and was named a 2013 Newsmaker of the year by the *Pittsburgh Tribune-Review*.

Acknowledgments

To my mother, Rosalie; my father, Bob; my Uncle Rich; our family friend Dr. Luke, and the rest of my technology-challenged friends and family. Without you, I would never have had to learn how to power wash a computer or to reconfigure a Wi-Fi network. You have stretched my abilities through necessity. Through my need to help all of you with your computer problems and semi-broken machines, I discovered the exciting world of technology. Heartfelt thanks just for being a part of my life.

My wife, Tiffeni, is the driving force of my life—always there, always solid, always supportive. Words cannot express my love and appreciation for your encouragement as we walk this journey together.

To my boys, Luke and Kyle, thank you for all of your support and love. I hope that you will find your own spark or passion in something, such as the passion I now have for technology and education.

Thanks to Pam Allyn for creating the framework that began my thinking about the reluctant reader. Her article, "Taming the Wild Text" is an amazing collection of ideas. She is such an inspiration to the world of reading. Her LitWorld project (www.litworld.org) advocates for literacy as a human right that belongs to all people. I both congratulate and thank her.

To the Scholastic family of Alan Boyko, Bill Barrett, Ann Lee, Don Small, Tony Hopkins, Larry Wissinger, Teryl McLane, Cheri Henderson, and Tracy Berger, I am so grateful to you all. Thank you for igniting my passion. Your constant support and friendship has been invaluable to me over the years. You are an amazing group of professionals.

Special thanks to Rebecca Turley. Thank you for your patience with me as I struggled with the right words to express my thoughts. I appreciate your support and talents.

To my social media friends, our professional learning community has been a driving force in the completion of this book. I always know that I can depend on your technological expertise to motivate and inspire new ways of thinking.

Finally, I offer my heartfelt thanks to God for my health, my happiness, and my family.

Dedication

I dedicate this book to my boys, Luke and Kyle Furman. Both reading and technology have been such an important and beautiful part of your lives. I simply cannot imagine the kind of fantastic technology you will experience in the future. Enjoy it.

Contents

Contents

Chapter 4

From Reluctance to Fluency 55

Appendix A

Apps to Inspire Even the Most
Reluctant Readers 71

Appendix B

ISTE Standards 79

Index 87

Introduction

The more you read, the more things you will know.
The more that you learn, the more places you'll go.

—DR. SUESS, *I CAN READ WITH MY EYES SHUT!*

This is a powerful time of change, with creativity and innovation leading the way. Conformity is outdated. We are raising digital-age learners who challenge us to update the way we communicate, the way we learn, and certainly the way we teach. Using technologies that we have yet to conceive, our students will be the next generation of creative thinkers and problem solvers—tomorrow's eBay founders and Facebook creators.

Who are the creators, those innovative and out-of-the-box thinkers? They are the insatiable learners. They are readers. But it is essential that we do more than merely encourage our students to read. We must also introduce them to innovative ways of exploring new things, and it is technology that enables this.

The sheer volume of information available at our fingertips via technology is simply mind-blowing. The platforms through which we are able to explore and learn are ever changing and often complex. This book was written to help you better understand today's technology so that you, in turn, may provide students with the tools they need to be successful.

Technology now demands that our students be both proficient learners and proficient readers. These skills are intricately connected, and they are vital in transforming young learners into innovative adults who can compete in the marketplace of ideas.

But what about reluctant readers? What is unique about them, and what stands in the way of their success? *Reluctant reader* is a term that educators toss around quite a bit, although sometimes not accurately. Google defines the word *reluctant* as: unwilling and hesitant; disinclined.

Based on this definition, we could describe a reluctant reader as someone who has not found an interest in reading—that intrinsic motivation that comes with reading for pleasure or for gaining knowledge. In other words, the reluctant reader simply has no desire or interest to read, and who does not often see the purpose or worth in reading. A typical thought of a reluctant reader may be, "Why read a book when I can watch a movie or find the information I need on a computer?"

A reluctant reader, however, should not be confused with a struggling reader; these two learners are quite different. A struggling reader has difficulty reading and is often a reluctant reader because of it. After all, who wants to do something they have difficulty accomplishing? A reluctant reader can accomplish the task just fine; they just choose not to begin. Therefore, our focus here is on the reader who has found neither the desire nor the interest to read. Our challenge is to help reluctant readers find a spark of interest that gives them that intrinsic fire to pick up a book, start reading, and, more important, *keep* reading.

Digital-Age Jobs
Demand Digital-Age Skills

Our technology-driven world has reached a point where a high school diploma no longer guarantees middle class status. Blue collar jobs are rapidly diminishing, while technology-focused professions evolve and multiply. It is more important than ever that individuals read with great proficiency. Being illiterate 50 years ago did not automatically doom young adults because an abundance of blue collar jobs were available to them. Many of today's jobs that provide gainful employment to reluctant readers may very well be gone by the time those students enter the workforce.

Technology, Reading,
and the Shrinking World

Through technology our world is actually shrinking. We can turn on our laptops or tablets and communicate with anyone in the world at a moment's notice. I can recall a time when this wasn't possible. I've seen technology change and take this shape over the course of my life. Our students, of course, have been born into a world that provides easy access to this virtual environment. They can and do collaborate and communicate with colleagues from almost anywhere in the world in ways that were unimaginable even a generation ago. Even so, students need help to safely and productively navigate this fast-changing virtual world. This is why it is essential that we equip our students with the digital-age skills they need. We must help them become independent readers who can serve as excellent communicators of knowledge.

Cross-Disciplinary Thinking

Today's success stories often involve cross-disciplinary thinkers who successfully jump traditional boundaries between disciplines. As we continue the move to a technology-driven society, our digital-age learners will be required to blend a number of technical and nontechnical considerations so that they may navigate their way around a number of disciplines successfully. In other words, it is no longer acceptable to assume that a student's strength in the sciences or in math can make up for his or her lack of skill in language arts. Regardless of an individual's chosen profession, technology demands that each be an excellent communicator of knowledge. And to do so a student needs to be a proficient reader.

The Art of Information Literacy

Surviving and thriving in the current knowledge economy demands excellent communication skills, and these skills ultimately come from an exceptional reading ability.

Social currency in this new world is nearly as important as financial wealth. Today's success stories are often about people who are financially successful because of their social currency in the virtual world. Here again, reading serves as the foundation of one's knowledge and reputation as a subject matter expert.

Technology Standards

Educators today have to ensure that they teach multiple competencies and touch on multiple standards. This is not an easy job, given the constraints of time and the sheer volume of content to teach. Thankfully, online tools allow teachers to combine the concepts of reading and digital literacy seamlessly so they can teach both at the same time. This provides students the opportunity to meet technology benchmarks, such as those outlined by the International Society for Technology in Education, while they learn to read.

For example, by combining traditional teaching strategies for reading with the tech tools detailed in this book, students should be able to:

- Flex their creative thinking skills

- Enhance their ability to work collaboratively with other students

- Improve their ability to apply digital tools to gather and utilize the information they obtain

- Conduct research, manage projects, and solve problems

- Demonstrate their fluency in technology concepts, systems, and operations

Blending Great Books and Today's Technology

As avid book readers know, finishing a book often leaves them with a sense of accomplishment. To experience this, readers first must find books about something that piques their interest. In the next chapter, we will examine the challenges students have with this first step and explore ways technology can help educators easily find great books that students will love. From there, we will consider great technology tools designed to help students discuss what they've read, share their books, and develop social currency through creative work that is based on the literature they've come to know.

It's worth mentioning that there are countless apps designed to help pre-readers, early readers, and readers with disabilities. There are also a plethora of apps that can help individuals improve their writing, comprehension, vocabulary, grammar, and spelling skills. While this book primarily focuses on online tools, Appendix A, "Apps to Inspire Even the Most Reluctant Readers," provides a robust list of apps that can help students build specific language skills.

Chapter 1

Help Me Find a Book

There are many little ways to enlarge your child's world. Love of books is the best of all.

—JACQUELINE KENNEDY

AS A PRINCIPAL, I often observe my classrooms in a casual manner, finding it best to take a backseat to the learning process that is underway. One day I walked into a classroom when the students were engaged in silent, sustained reading. Noticing me, the teacher walked over and whispered, "This is a waste of 30 minutes. Half the kids aren't even reading." I was immediately concerned because, as educators, we never want to waste 30 minutes in a day. I looked at the teacher and said that perhaps it was time we consider why our kids aren't reading. The teacher looked surprised, although I think she knew where I was going. I explained that we can't expect our young students to know how to find a good book—and we certainly can't expect them to develop a love of reading—if we don't provide them with the inspiration for doing so.

To get a better idea of why our students aren't reading and understand why they often wander aimlessly through the library's aisles, try this experiment: Ask your students about the newest kids' movies, video games, and television programs. They will likely rattle off an extensive list. This should come as no surprise, considering that young people are inundated with ads and information about the latest movies, games, and TV shows on a daily basis.

Next, ask your students to name some of the latest children's books on the market. They may very well meet you with a look of confusion or silence. After all, when was the last time there was a commercial or advertisement about a book? Books aren't typically marketed as heavily as other forms of media, so students are often completely unaware of the newest offerings in the literary world.

Because many students are not enjoying a rich exposure to books, it is no wonder they don't know what interests them in the literary world. After all, students can't be interested in something they don't even know exists!

This is where educators must enter the picture. We must help students find books that will excite them. In essence, we must become their personal librarians!

As Barbara Moss and Terrell A. Young, the authors of *Creating Lifelong Readers through Independent Reading* (2010), put it:

One of your most important responsibilities is to help students catch the desire to read. Some students achieve this on their own, but a great many do not. Virtually all students can benefit from the enthusiasm, interest, and expertise of an adult—teacher, parent, or librarian—who knows children's books. Heightening the students' awareness of the exhilarating possibilities of print can acquaint them with a jolt of literature and provide them with a love of reading that may last a lifetime.

> I like mystery and action books because they make you want to keep reading.
>
> —ADAM, 6TH GRADE

For the Love of Reading

Think you can't find great kid's books and online tools that will awaken the love of reading in your students? Think again. Several great web-based resources are designed to do just that.

Book Wizard

Searching for books your students will love is easy with Book Wizard (www.scholastic.com/bookwizard). This free web-based tool allows teachers to break down a huge catalog of children's books into manageable groups that match their school's reading system and their students' reading levels and interests. Best of all, Book Wizard is fully customizable, allowing teachers to refine their search once they discover something they like.

Book Wizard has more than 50,000 children's books in its system from all publishers; it doesn't limit teachers to only books published by Scholastic. However, if teachers want to add books to their classroom library, they can refine their Book Wizard search to include all titles that are available for purchase through Scholastic.

Teachers can get Book Wizard up and running in minutes without an account. However, by creating an account, the service can save searches and remember your particular reading level settings. Those with a Book Wizard account can also create and save their own customized book lists. These lists can be printed, or they can be provided to students and parents online.

Book Wizard is simple to use. A large search box is located at the top of the page, and features three different search options:

- *All Books:* This quick search allows you to search all books in the system by author, keyword, or concept

- *Similar Books:* This BookAlike search allows you to enter a familiar title to find books of a similar topic or genre

- *Reading Level:* This search parameter helps you find books categorized by different reading levels and systems

To keep your search simple, choose the All Books tab and then select the type of leveled system your school uses. Book Wizard can search by four of the most commonly used reading level systems:

- Grade level equivalent

- Guided reading (A–Z)

- Developmental Reading Assessment (A, 1–80)

- Lexile Measure (200L–1600L)

To conduct a keyword search in All Books, simply enter a word (or term), such as "vampires," into the search field. Typing in a word will bring up a list of suggestions that you may use to refine your search further. Once you have finished entering keywords, click Find Books. Book Wizard then searches for books and brings up a comprehensive list based on your search criteria.

The search results in Book Wizard provide a wealth of information for each book, including title, author, interest level, grade level equivalent, and genre. You can get more information about a specific book, including synopsis and author information, by clicking on its cover art or title. Search results also show whether a book is in any reading motivation programs, such as Scholastic Reading Counts! and Accelerated Reader.

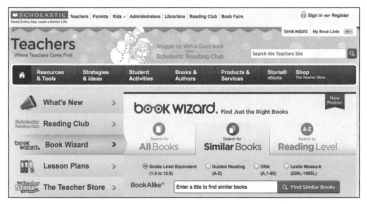

Figure 1.1 Book Wizard features some ready-made book lists on specific themes, such as Thanksgiving, Veterans Day, and books similar to those in a popular series, like *The Hunger Games.*

At this point, Book Wizard provides you with yet another opportunity to refine your search. On the left-hand side of the search results page, a Browse By bar allows you to choose books based on a different reading level, theme/ subject, genre, and series. You can also sort your results alphabetically by author or title. Once you find a book, the Add to Book List feature allows you to assemble your own recommended list.

If you use multiple devices, you can use the Book Wizard Mobile app to synchronize your data within Scholastic accounts, allowing you to keep your book lists current even when you are away from your personal computer.

You also have the option to choose BookAlike at this stage and continue your search using a handy tool at the top of the search results that allows you to adjust the reading level by sliding an arrow right or left.

I like books where you can't predict
what's going to happen next.

—ALEX, 4TH GRADE

Listbuilder

Listbuilder (http://listbuilder.scholastic.com) offers users a
way to search for Scholastic books that align with educational standards commonly used by all 50 U.S. states. For
example, teachers can browse the Common Core State
Standards, organized by subject and grade level, to see
correlations between them and Scholastic titles.

Figure 1.2 Listbuilder's Common Searches feature creates lists of the top
100 titles in a variety of categories, such as best books for boys, multicultural
books, and favorite authors.

There is a host of ways to search within Listbuilder, making this site extremely user-friendly. For example, the Advanced Title search allows teachers to search by the following:

- Keywords
- Genre
- Theme
- Type (fiction, nonfiction, book collections, instructional support programs, and more)
- Reading levels (grade, age, accelerated reader, guided reading, DRA, and so forth)
- Formats (hardcover, paperback, big books, audio, video, and others)
- Dewey Number
- Bilingual
- Books with Accelerated Reading Quizzes
- Books with Scholastic Reading Counts!
- Books with Reviews
- Books with Awards
- State Standard Correlations
- Publication Date

By signing up for Listbuilder's free service, you can create and build your own list and place orders. Teachers and librarians may choose to order entire book collections or individual titles.

Goodreads

Goodreads (www.goodreads.com) is an exceptional platform that students can use to engage with others about the books they've read. The site also provides a number of features that allow educators to gain insight on what their students are reading. Teachers can use Goodreads to do the following:

- Track the books their students are reading, have read, or want to read through the virtual Bookshelves feature

- Use the site's recommendation engine to provide suggestions tailored to a student's interests

- Learn more about the books that children are reading through community reviews

- Communicate with other teachers to share information about titles that students have enjoyed

Teachers can browse books by category, and they can use the site's search feature to search by title, author, or International Standard Book Number (ISBN). Goodreads also provides a fantastic array of lists, including the Goodreads Choice Awards: The Best Books of 2014.

Goodreads allows users to search by specific genres and view a list of the most popular or newly released books within that genre. This is a useful feature for teachers who want to know what students of a given age are reading.

Another helpful feature on Goodreads is Listopia, which allows users to search books based on what other folks have said about them. For example, a Listopia search within the Children's Books category will yield a number of interesting subsections, such as "Which books got you hooked?" and "Favorite books from my childhood."

In addition to viewing what other folks think about books, you can join in on the fun by voting for your favorite books or rate the books chosen in a particular subsection. Just choose one of the subsections within Children's Books to get started. In addition to voting for the books within these subsections, you may also click the Want to Read button associated with each title. Doing so adds the title to your virtual bookshelf so you can order it or reference it later.

Other List Services

If you're looking for a quick list of suggestions, a number of websites keep running lists of the newest and most popular children's books. Here are a few of my favorites:

- The American Library Association (www.ala.org) publishes recommended reading lists; search for ALA Reading Lists

- Oprah.com (www.oprah.com) has a useful reading list that separates suggested books into age groups and categories

- Readkiddoread (www.readkiddoread.com) provides information about recommended books by age groups and categories (illustrated books, transitional books, page-turners, and advanced reads); this site even has an I-Hated-to-Read-Til-I-Read-This Booklist for Boys list

- The International Reading Association (www.reading.org) provides an appealing reading list; children evaluate the books listed and write reviews

Storia

If your classroom is shifting to ebooks, you may be interested in Storia (www.teacher.scholastic.com/ereading-resources), a free interactive e-reading application that students can use at school or at home on a variety of desktop computers and mobile devices. Storia provides users with access to a growing collection of ebooks for a wide range of reading levels and genres. The app's library is tailored for students ages 3–14, with customizations for younger and older readers. Primary-level ebooks include audio recordings that read the entire book aloud to a beginning reader. More experienced readers can also use text-to-speech technology to hear books. All Storia books come with a dictionary feature and note-taking and highlighting tools.

Teachers can use the app for individual and small group reading on touch tablets, or for whole class instruction by projecting Storia onto a whiteboard. Best of all, Storia comes with reports that allow teachers to monitor their students' reading progress.

Figure 1.3 Storia is an interactive, educational e-reading application specifically designed for students. The free app comes with read-aloud capabilities and enrichment activities that aim to build fun and learning into literacy programs.

Social Media for Educators

Social media is an excellent platform through which teachers can share information about where to find appropriate literature for children. There are many online communities dedicated to finding good literature for kids. If you explore social media sites, you will soon discover that social media is a fantastic way to bring professional educators together, whether across town or across the country. Teachers can participate in them to learn from one another about what literature is working, what isn't working, and what might work in the future.

Pinterest

We have just three professional development days each year in my school. As a principal, I am always on the lookout for opportunities to assist my teachers beyond those precious few professional development days. The challenge is to introduce something that is appropriate for all of my teachers—from those fresh from college to those with more than 40 years of experience.

Using the ingenious social media site Pinterest (www. pinterest.com), I created a professional learning network (PLN) and dedicated a half-day of professional development to the PLN. I had every teacher create an account, link to each other, and share a group board. This created a 24/7 professional development platform.

My goal was to provide common ground where teachers could gather information from other social media sites and share it with one another. To my great satisfaction, the PLN worked wonderfully right from the start. Now, any time a teacher finds a good book or a good source of information, they can pin it onto their Pinterest board, which then immediately sends it to everyone's Pinterest boards in the PLN. For example, if I come across a new book or resource I want to share, I simply pin it to my Pinterest board, and my teachers receive it instantaneously. It's instant professional development for the educator! On many occasions, I've had the enjoyment of walking into school and hearing teachers talk about something I placed on Pinterest just the night before.

Figure 1.4 Pinterest is a visual discovery tool teachers can use to share ideas. Users create and share collections of visual bookmarks (boards) by selecting an image, webpage, or website, and then pinning it to an existing or newly created board.

Twitter

At a recent conference, a teacher asked me, "How can I give my students choices when they can't find a book?" Although there are a number of ways to go about doing this, I suggested they pose a question on Twitter (www. twitter.com). This network is a fantastic source for posing a question and getting many responses, quickly and conveniently.

Twitter is a unique social media experience that limits communication between people to just a short blurb of

140 characters or less. Such a blurb is called a tweet. Hashtags—searchable keywords or a sequence of characters prefixed with the pound sign (#)—are what make Twitter incredibly useful for finding and sharing information. The hashtag allows users to search for information pertinent to a specific topic of conversation on Twitter. For example, you might search Twitter with the hashtag #summerreading to find out what others are saying about summer reading. Chances are that such a search will deliver a number of useful ideas and lists, including the newest or most popular books for fun summer reading.

Twitter is also a fantastic resource for allowing users to connect with authors and other significant people in the realm of children's literature, and for finding to-the-point reviews on books. Many popular children's authors have their own Twitter accounts, including Jeff Kinney (@wimpykid), the author of *Diary of a Wimpy Kid,* and Kate Messner (@KateMessner), author of such popular books as *Eye of the Storm* and *Capture the Flag.* Another notable contributor to Twitter is Pam Allyn (@pamallyn), a children's rights and literary advocate, and author of several books for parents and teachers.

LinkedIn

LinkedIn (linkedin.com) has myriad groups for professional educators who use the platform to communicate with one another. Most professional educational organizations have LinkedIn accounts that offer teachers valuable insights on any number of current and relevant topics.

Here are a few LinkedIn groups worth joining:

- ASCD (Association for Supervision and Curriculum Development)
- NAESP (National Association of Elementary School Principals)
- Reader Leader Group
- Scholastic
- ISTE (International Society for Technology in Education)

Technology Standards for Teachers

As technology integration continues to increase in our society, it is paramount that teachers possess the skills and behaviors of digital-age professionals. The tools, resources, and social networks discussed in this chapter not only support your efforts to get students reading, but also help you meet technology standards for educators.

The ISTE Standards for Teachers identifies several benchmarks you could successfully reach as you explore and experiment with the tools and strategies discussed so far. Some examples include modeling digital-age work and learning, promoting and modeling digital citizenship and responsibility, and engaging in professional growth and leadership by participating in global learning communities

(See Appendix B for more about the ISTE Standards for Teachers).

In the following chapter, we explore ways to give students an opportunity to demonstrate some of these proficiencies while they engage in book discussions with their peers.

Chapter 2

Help Me Discuss a Book

In the highest civilization, the book is still the highest delight. He who has once known its satisfactions is provided with a resource against calamity.

—RALPH WALDO EMERSON

READING HAS ALWAYS BEEN a thoroughly enjoyable experience for me. But, oftentimes, I love the discussions that follow the most. For example, my son and I recently watched *Percy Jackson and the Lightning Thief.* After the movie, my son suggested we read the series of books. My son read the first book, passed it on to me, and started on the second book. We continued this through all nine books of the series. Our conversations during this time were truly memorable, and so was the bonding experience we shared. We found ourselves talking about the books nearly every day, picking up in the morning where we left off the night before.

This was not the first time my family bonded over books. During my engagement to my lovely wife, we began reading the *Black Dagger Brotherhood* series by J. R. Ward. We spent months reading and talking about those books. They became the cornerstone of our nightly conversations. Fourteen years later, my wife and I still read many of the same books so that we can talk about them together.

What is the first thing you want to do after finishing a really good book? Chances are you want to discuss it with someone. And why not? Engaging in a dialogue about something you read is an enjoyable experience. We should assume that our students will want to do the same.

For the reluctant reader, the greatest reward may not merely lie in reading a good story and finishing a book. Rather, the big payoff for them may be in telling others about what they read. For this reason, we must engage reluctant readers beyond the book. In other words, once they have read the book and put it down, we may very well be met with a "now what?" sort of moment—the moment the book is finished, and the student is searching for validation. We must help them validate their reading experience. To do so, we must be armed with plenty of ideas, suggestions, and resources to help these students keep the joy of reading alive.

Giving students an opportunity to communicate with someone after reading a good book is one of the keys to creating a passion for reading. That passion—the desire to have a conversation about what they've read—is particularly important for reluctant readers. There is little chance these students will become motivated and inspired to read if they can't find lasting value in it. That is why it is important for educators to cultivate the feeling of excitement that reluctant readers feel when they get to share their thoughts with others who have read the same book. Fortunately, technology provides a number of fantastic platforms for doing so.

> I like when people say I am so good at reading and they ask me to read to them.
>
> —LILY, 3RD GRADE

Social Currency

Social currency—the act of sharing information to encourage future encounters—helps us feel like we are relevant, participating members of a given group. Although social currency is not a new concept, the internet certainly facilitates its use.

If we can find a good book for our reluctant readers, and then find technology platforms through which they can share their thoughts about what they've read, chances are that these students will begin to feel more relevant. They will feel that they have amassed some social currency through reading.

Paying close attention to how we nurture the social currency of our reluctant readers is often a critical component in our efforts to transform these students into independent readers. Giving young readers a sense that they know about a book, and that they are not the only ones who feel a certain way about a book, is a powerful tool for creating a passion for reading. The conversation that occurs after people read a book is the link between reading and social currency. It's powerful and it's effective!

Goodreads

Goodreads (www.goodreads.com) certainly hits the mark when it comes to social currency. Sure, motivating reluctant readers is about finding books that interest them (via services like Book Wizard and Listbuilder). But helping these students feel as though they are relevant members of a community is an even bigger motivator. If students feel isolated, or if they feel as if reading won't improve their social currency, it may be a long, uphill battle for the teachers who are attempting to motivate them.

Launched in 2007, Goodreads claims to be the largest site for readers and book recommendations. As of the writing of this book, Goodreads now boasts 30 million members, 900 million books, and 34 million reviews.

Goodreads provides a social experience where reluctant readers can share their thoughts and ideas with others who have read the same book. Students can engage in lively online conversations, make quizzes, and take quizzes from others who have read the same book. It's a literary world within itself, where reluctant readers feel as if they aren't alone. Goodreads brings children together from the same peer group, providing them with a virtual community where reading is exciting and where talking about a book is as much fun as reading it.

For example, many discussions are currently taking place about *The Hunger Games*. Tens of thousands of readers have joined in. Users may join in on the existing games, quizzes, and conversations within these discussions, or they may choose to start a new book discussion.

For users who choose to start a new discussion, a new window pops up, allowing them to post a question, a game idea, a quiz, or a viewpoint, and then share it with others.

Teachers can create a dedicated book group within Goodreads that only their students can join. Students can use this group to start discussions about the books they are currently reading, and join in on current discussions within that group. By having these discussions online, students can easily converse about their books at any time, whether at school or at home.

Goodreads is a great place to encourage students to join a specific group, start a group and ask others to join it, or simply read what others are saying about current topics. To start, users should visit the Groups page (www.goodreads.com/group).

Students and teachers can even pose a question to the Goodreads community. A question such as, "Can someone recommend a humorous book about baseball?" will generate a slew of great replies.

ePals

ePals (www.epals.com) is a social network designed for the K–12 learner. It is a meeting place where teachers and students from nearly anywhere in the world can gather to discuss literature. Their website states that more than half a million classrooms in more than 200 countries and territories have become members of the ePals Global Community. The excitement of discussing a book with another classroom—whether across town or across the world—is unmatched in terms of motivating reluctant readers.

Teachers can search by keyword, student age, language, country, and number of students to find a classroom on ePals. Moreover, they can choose the type of collaboration they would like to have with another classroom, including email exchange or Skype/video chat.

One of the easiest ways to begin collaborating with others through ePals is by utilizing the ePals Project Experience. This feature allows teachers to either begin a collaborative project (by creating one of the site's Project Ideas) or to join another teacher's project. If a teacher creates a project, and the project is approved through ePals, a Project Workspace is created. This project is then added to the Join Project area where others can view it and request to join. But teachers don't have to wait for others to find their project; they can utilize the Finding Classroom service to invite other classes to join them.

Through Project Experience, teachers can search by project and narrow their search by language, student age, keyword, country, project type, project duration, common core area of interest, or collaboration preference.

ePals also has a number of popular Learning Centers, where students can engage in fun activities, games, and discussions.

> When I read a magical book
> I feel like I'm in a magical place.
>
> —CARA, 2ND GRADE

Videoconferencing

Technology allows students in one school to videoconference with students in other schools. Through such platforms as Skype (www.skype.com), ooVoo (www.oovoo.com), and FaceTime for Mac (www.apple.com/mac/facetime) students can talk face to face from virtually anywhere in the world. This is a great way for young readers to share their thoughts and ideas while gleaning new insights and perspectives from their peers.

To a fifth grade reluctant reader, for example, a story about an Irish immigrant may not seem that riveting. However, the same book may become quite an interesting read if that student has the opportunity to engage in dialogue with students from Ireland.

Because perspectives on a story may be decidedly different from students in another country, videoconferencing can open up the door for exciting and thought-provoking discussions. Keep in mind that videoconferencing needn't be overly complicated or difficult! Teachers can just as easily videoconference with a neighboring school district. Videoconferencing is simply a technology that can allow students to interact with people they may have otherwise never met, be it with students half a world away or just down the hall.

Skype

With Skype, (http://education.skype.com), users can make video and voice calls to anyone else with a Skype account, regardless of where participants are located. Skype users also enjoy instant messaging and file sharing, all of which are free of charge. For a nominal fee, users can also make group calls, connecting up to 10 people on one call.

Figure 2.1 Teachers can use Skype on a variety of devices, including smartphones, computers, and televisions with the Skype program installed.

To use Skype, you will need a webcam, an internet connection (a broadband connection is preferred), and a computer or mobile device with a speaker and microphone.

ooVoo

ooVoo is a videoconferencing tool that allows video chat with up to 12 users at once. Through ooVoo, users can send video messages to other ooVoo members, record and upload messages to YouTube, and instant message others. ooVoo provides free video chat, free video messaging, free phone calls, and free instant messaging.

You can download ooVoo on a PC, Mac, Android device, iPhone, or iPad.

FaceTime for Mac

iPhone, iPad, and iPod users can take advantage of FaceTime, which is a service that allows users to video-conference with one another for free between Mac/Apple devices. Videoconferencing with another classroom is relatively easy with FaceTime. To get started, users simply need an Apple ID and an email address. Users can click on a phone number or email address in their contacts to begin a session.

Children's Authors Network!

The Children's Authors Network! (canetwork.weebly.com) connects students with some of today's favorite authors, and is another great way that teachers can use videoconferencing to encourage reluctant readers to engage in books. Many times, the free videoconferencing sessions on this network follow a question-and-answer format, providing students with the chance to get inside the mind of an author.

Using this network, our school found an author from the Boston area. We were able to arrange a Skype session for a 20-minute Q&A about a book that our students had just read. The author was so encouraged by the excellent questions our students were asking that she extended the session, even reading a portion of her next book that had yet to be released! The class was spellbound, and the excitement of being able to talk with an author who writes books that are important in their lives was a special experience, both for the students and for us.

Google+ Hangouts

Google+ Hangouts (plus.google.com/hangouts) has become a dominant video chat resource, thanks to its interactive capabilities that allow many people to chat at one time. It also works seamlessly with other Google apps, including Google Drive, Google Docs, and Google Calendar.

Google+ Hangouts has also become a popular platform for many internet television shows because of its effortless, screen-sharing features.

Google+ Hangouts is a part of Google for Education (www.google.com/edu), a collection of productivity tools, class content, and other resources for learning and teaching. Google Docs are widely used in schools, making Google+

Hangouts a good option because so many already have Gmail accounts. In addition, because Chromebooks are popular in schools and Google is native to Chromebooks, many teachers find that using Google+ Hangouts is a convenient option.

Virtual Book Clubs

Book clubs, often referred to as reading groups, are simply groups of readers who get together to discuss books and other forms of literature. Thanks to the internet, book clubs have evolved into virtual book clubs that allow people from any part of the world to participate in interesting and spirited discussions.

Virtual book clubs are yet another great way that teachers can help reluctant readers become excited about books. These clubs provide online platforms where students can voice their opinions and learn more about a book with the input of other readers.

LitLovers

Teachers can create a virtual book club using a variety of platforms. A single classroom can participate in a particular book club, or it can be available to a national audience. LitLovers (www.litlovers.com) publishes a comprehensive index of reading group guides and provides links to some of the most popular book clubs on the internet. LitLovers makes it easy for users to find both general interest and special interest book clubs, and it provides teachers with a plethora of helpful hints for starting their own.

One of my fourth grade teachers always has his class read the Shakespeare play, *A Midsummer Night's Dream.* To make this assignment interesting, he sets up a blog and asks his students to join the forum as one of the characters from the play! The blog starts when he poses a question about the play on the blog and the students, in character, answer the question. Using LitLovers as inspiration, this teacher found a unique way to encourage his students to dive deeper into the content of the story.

Edublogs

For teachers who want to start their own virtual book club for their classroom, Edublogs (http://edublogs.com) is a popular platform. This site, which touts itself as "the world's most popular education blogging service," allows teachers to create and manage a blog for book discussions. Thanks to this site's user-friendly features, teachers can get a blog up and running in minutes. The site's security features allow teachers to monitor and moderate all of the content posted by their students.

Email

Email is one of the simplest ways to start a virtual book club. Email encourages users to read, and it certainly encourages them to write! This platform is often quite effective at improving our reluctant reader's communication skills. And, because reading and writing support one another, the act of combining these activities through email can be a very effective way to encourage independent reading.

Email correspondence through online communities, such as ePals, gives students the opportunity to use a single tool to communicate with a classroom across the country, world, or simply on the other side of town. Moreover, writing an email encourages reluctant readers to create a message that is organized and written in a meaningful manner. The act of composing an email, sending it, and then reading an email in reply is an exciting prospect for many students. Such an experience may very well be the impetus for the reluctant reader to engage more deeply in reading.

Think about the excitement you could generate if your classroom in Massachusetts had a book conversation on the American Revolution with a classroom in England! How about connecting your classroom in Pennsylvania with a classroom in Alabama to discuss a book on slavery? What about discussing mythological stories of Perseus Jackson with a classroom in Greece? The dynamics that teachers can create through email communication is fascinating!

> You never know, some people
> may like the same books as you!
>
> —SARAH, 3RD GRADE

Digital Citizenship

Virtual book clubs, including those that use email and blogging, provide teachers with the perfect opportunity to talk about digital citizenship (also often referred to as digital wellness or digital ethics). Digital citizenship is a concept that involves the importance of teaching students about the responsible use of technology; that abusing technology has immediate and long-lasting effects; and that once you publish something on the internet, it's memorialized there forever.

Students with an awareness and appreciation for digital citizenship understand the powerful relationship between technology and human, cultural, and societal issues. Teachers have a duty to talk to their students about the responsible use of technology, particularly if they are involved in using any type of technology with their students. Thankfully, there are numerous resources available to guide these discussions. For example, the ISTE Standards for Students (See Appendix B) offer four objectives for students as they learn how to practice appropriate behavior online:

- Advocate and practice the safe, legal, and responsible use of information and technology

- Exhibit a positive attitude toward using technology that supports collaboration, learning, and productivity

- Demonstrate personal responsibility for lifelong learning

- Exhibit leadership for digital citizenship

Here are some other resources about digital citizenship that you might find helpful:

- Digital Citizenship—Using Technology Appropriately (www.digitalcitizenship.net) is a resources page designed to help teachers show students why digital citizenship is important. This site features nine themes of digital citizenship, which can serve as a jumping-off point for beneficial conversations between teachers and students.

- Common Sense Media (www.commonsensemedia. org) is a nonprofit organization that partners with Knowledge Delivery Systems to provide a number of digital citizenship online courses for school districts.

- Cable in the Classroom—Teaching Digital Citizenship (www.ciconline.org/DigitalCitizenship) provides comprehensive information on online safety and security, digital literacy, and ethics and community.

In the next chapter, we will explore tools and resources that help students share books with others in a variety of engaging ways. Students can use these technologies to learn and demonstrate their abilities to summarize a book and, in turn, share great stories with their peers.

Chapter 3

Help Me Share a Book

A capacity and taste for reading gives access to whatever has already been discovered by others.

—ABRAHAM LINCOLN

MY SON (who happens to be the principal's kid) came home one evening with a poster board and announced, "I have to do a book report." I chuckled a bit as I looked at the poster board and said, "You can put the poster board down now; I have a different idea." My son laughed at that moment, too, because he knows how much I love technology. I took some time to familiarize him with a number of cool technologies, including GoAnimate (http://goanimate.com), an impressive animation tool that allows users to make scenes come to life. My son, who is a bit of a technology buff himself, wanted to take the idea of animation a step further by choosing a character from the book and setting up his animation as an interview between himself and his animated character. This, of course, required a bit of work on our part because the character would have to answer questions at the correct time as my son asked questions live in front of the classroom. Sneaking in and positioning myself at the back of the classroom on the day of his book report, I was so excited to see his project come to life. The awestruck looks on students' faces proved that the presentation was a success. I couldn't help but think how exciting it would be to engage the entire classroom in an activity such as this. And then I thought, why not?

For many children (and adults!), sharing their thoughts about a book once they have finished reading can be even more exciting and stimulating than the actual act of reading the book. The process of preparing and sharing can be quite gratifying. Sharing with others is, for many, the reward upon finishing a book.

My son's experience of sharing his book with his class certainly increased his social currency and made him feel satisfied and proud. The process of creating the project, and the eagerness with which he shared it, was exciting for me to witness. I can only imagine how pleased he must have felt upon seeing the reactions of his peers in class.

For reluctant readers who may have difficulty finding a reason to read a book, being able to anticipate the end result—to look forward to sharing it with others—may be the motivation they need to pick up a book and stick with it.

But beyond that, sharing literature with others has a dynamic ripple effect. The excitement a student puts forth when sharing a book is likely all that is needed to create excitement among others in the classroom. Sharing a book in a fun and creative way, and utilizing technology to do it, is a win-win situation for all. This is particularly true for a reluctant reader who is looking for more than the initial feeling of satisfaction upon finishing a book.

Educators play an important role in the ripple effect. They can create excitement in their classes by introducing students to the technology tools they, in turn, can use to share books with the class. Giving children something to look forward to—in the form of technology, which is a language most children speak fluently today—is often the motivating factor for getting them to read.

An effective way to keep the momentum going in your classroom is to introduce your children to the newest technology tools and to explore them together. Like so much other education-based technology out there, these technologies are often free and easily available to anyone with an internet connection.

Before introducing your children to the latest technology tools for sharing books, research a few and determine which ones work best for your students' ages and abilities. Remember that introducing students to technology that is too advanced won't motivate them; instead, it will likely lead to discouragement and frustration, which will ultimately sabotage the effort.

Once you find a tech tool that interests you, get creative. Use it to make a book presentation of your own. Share it in class, upload it to your website, or share a link via email or a social media page. This demonstration should get students excited about working on their own book presentation project.

Provide parents with plenty of information about the project and the technology the students will be using. Furthermore, encourage parents to work alongside their children and monitor their activities while online.

Following are some of the latest technology tools to introduce to your students to get them to share their books, with imagination and innovation leading the way.

> Reading takes you on adventures in your mind.
>
> —LEXA, 4TH GRADE

Video Book Talks

Video book talks are one of the simplest ways to use technology to get kids engaged in reading. There is a plethora of book talks online (YouTube, Scholastic, and similar sites) that can be a great source of inspiration, both for teachers and students.

A great way to use technology to create a fun book talk is to ask your students to create a movie-like trailer for their book. Because children are barraged with movie trailers on television and in movie theaters, they will already understand the concept. You can ask students to consider what a trailer would look and sound like for their book. Ask them to create an exciting trailer that will get others interested enough to read their book (without giving too much of the storyline or ending away).

A great way to keep the momentum going in your classroom is to limit the trailer to just two minutes, thereby keeping students interested while also challenging them to get their classmates' attention.

The objective of a student-led book talk is to create enough excitement to encourage classmates to want to pick up the book and read it too. A good trailer introduces a book, engages viewers with a few tidbits of interesting information, and then ends with an exciting cliffhanger that leaves the class wanting more.

Allow students to make their book trailers fun and interesting by using costumes, props, and even sound effects! Give them time to record their book trailer in class if they don't otherwise have access to a video recorder.

Present the book trailers during class or make it an event by airing them as part of the morning's announcements. Upload them to your website or social media page, and encourage students to share their book trailers with family and friends.

Scholastic has an extensive list of book talks made by Scholastic staff members and others that may be a great source of inspiration, both for you and your students (See Figure 3.1 on page 46.)

Figure 3.1 The Scholastic website features a variety of book previews, author interviews, and book recommendations by celebrities such as iCarly star Miranda Cosgrove and music star Taylor Swift.

Animated Book Talks

Kids love technology, and they love animation. Combining the two is a recipe for a sure hit. Students can use animation sites to create fantastic book talks in nearly any format. Teachers may want to choose the format or let students flex their creative muscles and use a site of their choosing to produce a book recap, create a book trailer, or bring a part of the book to life.

It seems as though a new free site for creating animation appears every day. Currently, one of the most popular for the education market is GoAnimate.

GoAnimate

GoAnimate is ideal for children because it enables them to be creative even if they don't possess many technical skills. This user-friendly site allows users to either create a completely customized animated book talk or choose from the site's library of existing objects (probably the best way to go for young readers). Users can choose a soundtrack from the site, upload a soundtrack of their choice, have a computerized voice speak the dialogue, or record the dialogue themselves.

Figure 3.2 GoAnimate for Schools provides characters, backgrounds, and props that are appropriate for a K–12 audience. Weapons, alcohol, or violent actions are not available.

GoAnimate provides an area where teachers can go to create a school account for their students, giving them a secure environment to create animated book talks. All of the videos within a school account are moderated and managed, and only school-safe content is available to the students. Although creating a school account is not free, GoAnimate does have a "try before you buy" feature.

Comic Strips

Many teachers are now turning to comic strips to engage their students. Teachers at my school love the idea of helping their students create comic strips about books, as this activity provides them with the visual stimuli they crave. This activity also effectively bridges the gap between school work and leisure time, meaning that students are motivated to create comics.

Comic strips are a high-interest medium and have been shown to motivate and engage reluctant readers. Indeed, comics provide an excellent platform for students to flex their creative- and critical-thinking skills, all while developing their visual and media literacy skills.

Following are some of my favorite technologies that can help students make comics.

Bitstrips for Schools

Bitstrips for Schools (www.bitstripsforschools.com) is an online comic strip program that allows students to create their own comic strips. Teachers can create private, virtual classrooms that students access with a code. This ensures that students have a safe work environment to get creative.

To use Bitstrips for Schools, teachers simply sign up, create a virtual classroom, and provide students with their own private passwords to enter the site. Once the virtual classroom is up and running, teachers can post an assignment for the students to create, either at home or at school. Once comic strips are completed, students can leave feedback for each other and publish comments for the classroom to see. A book assignment can quickly turn into a creative project using Bitstrips for Schools and, because it allows students to interact and collaborate with one another, their social currency is nourished.

Make Beliefs Comix

Make Beliefs Comix (www.makebeliefscomix.com) is another free website that allows students to make their own comic strips. Because it offers fewer features than Bitstrips for Schools, Make Beliefs Comix is ideal for younger students.

Figure 3.3 Make Beliefs Comix offers teacher-submitted lesson plans, writing tools, and a variety of activities designed for students with special needs.

To use the tool, students simply choose how many panels they want to create on their comic strip and which characters they want to use. This website allows students to create comic dialogue bubbles to give their characters a voice, and it provides a number of different backgrounds and characters to play with.

Pixton

Pixton (www.pixton.com) offers Pixton for Schools, a unique and secure spot for teachers and students to create, share, and publish comic strip stories. What makes Pixton unique is that it is also a social community that allows students to share their comic strips with students around the world.

Teachers can pair up with another classroom, read the same book, and have students make comic strips according to an assignment associated with the book. Once finished, students can share their comic strips with the other classroom, and from reading the comics of other classes discover what the others may have learned from the book. This type of activity often provides teachers with the perfect opportunity to open up lively classroom discussions.

Pixton markets its site as a pathway to literacy that captures students' attention and motivates them to learn. It is indeed a collaborative space that can foster interactions between students and teachers, and provides a visual learning experience that reinforces words with images. Pixton also has a lesson area that allows educators to share their lesson plans with other teachers.

Video Production

Teachers with older students (or more motivated students!) can take book presentations a step further by producing an entire video.

TouchCast

TouchCast (www.touchcast.com) is a fantastic app that provides students with a virtual news center format that allows them to make an advanced book report using web-based graphics and charts, text content, and images. This app does a great job of integrating video into the web experience, because it enables students to create videos and introduce web content within the clips. TouchCast is available for the iPad and for PCs using Windows 7.

Figure 3.4 TouchCast offers lesson plans, teacher-training resources, and an educator's guide for integrating its tool into the classroom.

Livestream

Livestream (http://new.livestream.com) allows students to create their own television shows about books. Unlike TouchCast, which produces a recorded video, Livestream produces a live broadcast (although it does have a number of archiving options), thus allowing teachers to set up their own channel. Simple Get Started and Sign Up for Free options allow users to get a Livestream channel up and running in a matter of minutes.

Once the channel is up, teachers may start an assignment by making their own book talk and airing it on their live stream channel. After students have watched it (and have become completely enamored with the technology), teachers can help students create their own Livestream book talks.

A great example of the use of Livestream is on International Literacy Day, a United Nations Educational, Scientific, and Cultural Organization (UNESCO) event, which occurs annually on September 8th. This live event brings together people from all over world, allowing them to come together virtually to share the same global reading experience.

Presentation Tools

Additional resources that offer your students a variety of platforms through which they can present their books are listed here. Providing a number of options allows students to utilize the platform that feels most comfortable to them (i.e., some students may prefer to write, while other students may prefer to use video). Following are some recommended sites:

- Authorstream (www.authorstream.com) is a platform for sharing PowerPoint presentations on the internet.

- Slideshare (www.slideshare.net) is an online community for sharing presentations.

- VoiceThread (www.voicethread.com) is a cloud application that allows users to upload, share, and discuss presentations, videos, images, audio files, and documents.

- Museum Box (http://museumbox.e2bn.org) allows users to create a virtual, three-dimensional "box" for book presentations.

- Glogster (http://edu.glogster.com) is a virtual version of a trifold poster or scrapbook.

- FlowVella Education (http://flowvella.com) is an iPad app that allows users to make interactive presentations by combining images, words, and video.

- Blogger.com (www.blogger.com) provides blogging templates, creation software, and an easy-to-use interface for publishing.

Reading Books and Reaching Benchmarks

As mentioned earlier, the tools and activities described in this book serve a dual purpose. While they help students discover a love of books, they can also help them reach important educational benchmarks, such as the Communication and Collaboration indicators found in the ISTE Standards for Students. For example, during the process of discussing and sharing a book with others through GoAnimate or TouchCast, young readers have an opportunity to show they can "communicate information and ideas effectively to multiple audiences using a variety of media and formats." (See Appendix B.)

In the next chapter, we continue our exploration of new tools and activities that highlight the rewards of reading while helping students develop higher-order thinking skills through analysis, evaluation, and creative writing.

Chapter 4

From Reluctance to Fluency

As a child, books were my transport. Through reading, I discovered worlds of people I had not known before. I read stories about history and places and people that moved me, reduced me to tears, brought me off of my couch and on a journey that never ended.

—PAM ALLYN

ROBERT WAS a reluctant reader. It wasn't that he couldn't read; it was that he had other priorities, like riding dirt bikes. After discovering this through a personal inventory quiz, Robert's teacher found a number of books through Book Wizard that she thought he would like. Knowing Robert had a touch tablet he used for gaming, his teacher contacted his parents and asked them to put the Storia app on Robert's device. She then purchased Robert's first ebook entitled, aptly enough, *Dirt Bike Racer,* and downloaded it onto his device. During the sustained reading time in class, Robert's teacher showed him how to begin reading his new ebook, which was filled with videos and pictures that interested him. It was the first time Robert had a positive experience reading a book. It was his "aha" moment, and he was hooked.

As Robert began reading more often, he became interested in finding books on his own. Using Goodreads he discovered many books about dirt bikes. He was becoming an avid reader.

A few months later, Robert's teacher asked him if he wanted to introduce his friends to the books he was reading. He said that he belonged to a BMX racing team, and that he would like to tell his teammates about the dirt bike books he really liked. His teacher helped him create and record book talks that he then began sharing on YouTube. He even used his bike to describe specific tricks and moves during his book talks. Robert quickly became a dirt bike expert among his circle of friends. He took his idea of posting dirt bike book talks a step further by creating his own web show called "Book Reviews for the Dirt Bike Rider."

Throughout Robert's journey, he learned that he not only had a passion for books but also that books could raise his social currency and allow him to take his love of dirt bikes to places he never thought possible. Robert's web show is now one of the most popular channels for young adult dirt bike riders.

How do you know, as an educator or parent, that your reluctant readers have come full circle and can now curate their own reading lives? The simple answer to this question may come when we see these students understand what they read, reflect on it, and then send their own ideas back out in the form of the written word.

Are your students simply reading, or are they reading, understanding, and creating? We all cheer when our students read, yet many of us don't understand that the cycle is not complete until new readers are able to communicate what they've read. To think critically and articulate thoughts is the academic form of expression, and students develop these abilities through the writing process.

We want students to seamlessly transition from reading to writing. In other words, we want them to realize that if they can think it, they can read it, and if they can read it, they can write it. In essence, if students can evaluate their reading, they have reached the highest form of reading.

> I like to read when it is quiet so I can let myself concentrate.
>
> —JACOB, 5TH GRADE

A Time for Reflection

Reflection conveys that readers have the ability to make judgments about what they have read. They can read it, they can argue it, and they can defend it. Reflection is exciting for students because they get to do something with a book after accomplishing the task of reading it. The activity gives students a sense that reading has a purpose. This is why it is crucial that educators work to ensure students have the opportunity to complete this process.

Reflection allows reluctant readers to ponder what they've read and look beyond. It is a time when new articles, books, and other types of written forms take shape. In short, reflection is part of a unique, cyclical process, an opportunity for students to read a book, reflect on it, and then create new material for someone else to read. A student may write a review of a book and a classmate may read it. If the classmate likes the review and decides to read the book, the process is set to begin again.

Personal reflection has a powerful effect on student achievement, and it is a time for students and teachers to relish. Taking what we've read, reflecting on it, and then turning around and giving our opinion or debating someone else's is considered a higher order of thinking. Any time we can get students to accomplish this level of thinking, we will broaden their minds and help them achieve.

Personal reflection and the creation of new thoughts and opinions after reading a book demonstrate the higher end of Bloom's taxonomy (See Figure 4.1.). The highest cognitive domains include evaluating (students' ability to make judgments about what they've read) and creating (when students can put together all of the parts to form a whole).

How do we get to the end stage, the creation? With a pen in hand—or fingers poised over the keyboard—of course.

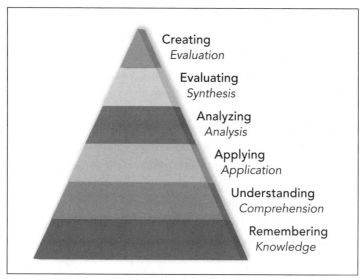

Figure 4.1 Bloom's taxonomy of learning.

The Pleasures of Writing

As educators we know that reading and writing go hand in hand. We all understand the importance of being able to express ourselves through the written word. But how do we actively encourage our students to begin communicating their thoughts and ideas via the written word? And how can technology facilitate this?

Using a variety of web-based resources, we can help our children flex their creative writing muscles, be it fiction or nonfiction. The abundance of resources on the internet provides students with a host of opportunities to reach the pinnacle of reading achievement through creative expression.

ePals Writing Center

The activities at ePals' The Writing Center (http://en. community.epals.com/student_creative_writing_center/ default.aspx) are a great place to start. Each activity is designed for students to do work on their own.

Express Yourself. The Express Yourself section of ePals, which highlights poetry, stories, songs, and narratives, is a great way for your students to connect with other students around the globe. Using this service, students can share their stories, poems, and narratives with others who also love words and creativity. This allows students to enjoy their favorite writing experiences and get inspired by other kids.

There are always great topics in play through Express Yourself that allow students to join in with others and engage in lively conversations. These topics might include the following:

- Write a story in three sentences
- Favorite poem or quote
- Need character ideas for sci-fi story
- Help me create a book!

Every Picture Tells a Story. The ePals team provides the writing inspiration for your students by way of a fun section called Every Picture Tells a Story. This section features photographs and a writing prompt, and your students do the rest!

Welcome to My Town! What's special about your town? Every town has something special, and this activity encourages students to become travel guides. Teachers can write a prompt that asks students to describe the unique features of the community in which they live. Once finished, students can publish their pieces on the ePals wiki.

Writers' Words Wiki. Because words are a writer's most powerful tool, choosing the right words can help readers on their writing quests. Writers' Words wiki helps students create a list of powerful words that can strengthen and enhance their own writing. This community forum allows students to add to each other's ideas and also add them to the ePals wiki page.

Art Stories. The ePals team does a fantastic job of using one creative form to inspire another. Art Stories are "short, art-inspired creative writing pieces" that allow student writers to work together to create an original story that is inspired by original artwork submitted by ePal members. An Art Stories activity provides interesting collaborative opportunities for students as they work together and inspire one another while writing the story.

> I like reading because reading is learning and I like learning.
>
> —ANNA, 4TH GRADE

Story Starters

A traditional writing prompt quickly becomes zany with
Scholastic's Story Starters (www.scholastic.com/teachers/
story-starters). This site features four story starter themes
that lead to a colorful casino-style slot machine that is sure
to attract young readers. By pulling on the arm and buttons
of the slot machine, students receive and refine story ideas
that the machine comes up with. And, the fun doesn't stop
there. Students can go on to electronically illustrate their
stories and print them in a charming format.

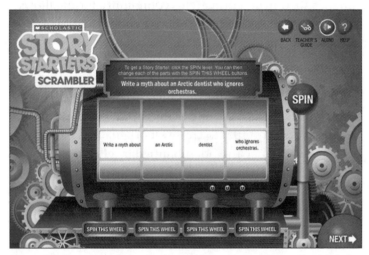

Figure 4.2 Story Starters is a student writing prompt that provides ideas for
character, plot, and setting.

The fun starts when your students (or you) choose a theme
for a story. Story Starters lets you choose an adventure,
fantasy, sci-fi, or scramble (a little bit of everything!).

Figure 4.3 All of Scholastic's Story Starters allow students to choose the appropriate theme before using the tool.

Once you choose your theme (we chose adventure), you then choose the grade level at which your students are writing. After having lots of fun spinning the dials, our machine came up with a lively adventure story prompt for a second grader: Describe a trip with a dotted pony who finds a hidden room!

Another spin of the wheel and our adventure story prompt turned into this: Write about a visit to the playground with a wise fish that travels to a faraway country!

Creative story prompts are sure to keep your students interested and engaged. Story Starters is easy to understand and the bright colors and fun sound effects are a fantastic way to attract the attention of even your most reluctant writers.

Student Blogging

Blogging has become one of the premiere technologies used to share and discuss information. We also know that reading and writing go hand in hand with the learning process. Blogging, then, allows students to engage in the learning process while also sharing their thoughts with a larger world. Further, blogs are a great platform for students who are interested in creative writing; after all, what better place to flex their creative writing skills than in a blog?

Bloggin' Around the World

Advanced student writers can become part of ePals international student blogging team called Bloggin' Around the World (www.epals.com) at no cost. Students can apply for a blog on either an individual or group (classroom) basis. Group bloggers can apply together and then blog on a rotating basis.

ePals is always looking for student bloggers who are enthusiastic, creative, and able to blog at least once a month throughout the academic year. The Student Blog page is also a great place for your students to read other student blogs.

Edublogs

Another great way introduce blogging to your classroom is through Edublogs (www.edublogs.org). I love Edublogs because it allows classrooms to really get the most out of the blogging experience. Following are some examples:

- Teachers can set up forums where students can interact with one another

- Teachers can quiz students through blogs, encourage feedback on classroom activities and projects, and provide students with a place to get the classroom help they need

- Students can create their own blogs and use them to express themselves as they would in a journal or open diary

- Students can create blogs that they can use as digital portfolios, uploading the projects they have created

- Students can use Edublogs to create their own student publications, such as a school newspaper

Figure 4.4 Edublog's free account provides 32 MB of space to write, create, and customize pages. The service is also ad free.

Edublogs serves as a social community and, instead of writing just for their teachers, students can write for a much larger audience. This opportunity often motivates students to publish their best work. Blogging also allows students to get immediate feedback on their work, and they can also provide others with feedback. In this way, students can create a collaborative atmosphere where they help each other improve as writers and readers.

Publishing

Publishing student writing online is a great way to get a class to read and take writing seriously. Students tend to put more effort into their writing if they know their peers will be reading it. Posting student work online for the world to see also provides students with a sense of pride because they can say that they are published writers. Teachers will appreciate this as an opportunity to discuss digital citizenship.

There are many websites that educators can use to encourage students to write and read each other's written work. The following sites are just a few of the many resources available.

Kids Are Authors

Kids Are Authors (www.scholastic.com/bookfairs/contest/kaa) is an annual competition through Scholastic that is open to students in kindergarten through eighth grade in the United States and in U.S. international schools. Scholastic designed this program as a way to encourage students to showcase their reading, writing, and artistic skills.

The program begins with a project coordinator and a team of three or more students who write and illustrate their own book. Using a collaborative, team-centered approach, students work together to communicate with one another, listen to each other's ideas, and edit their work. The team project is then submitted to Scholastic, who then publishes one book in fiction and one book in nonfiction. These books are then sold at Scholastic book fairs throughout the country.

The Students Are Authors program is a great way to inspire your students. Even if their book is not the winner in its category, students can nonetheless experience the sense of pride and satisfaction of seeing their book in a finished form.

Scholastic provides a host of information on their website about this annual program, including idea starters to get the students rolling on their project and a number of resources for encouraging and inspiring them.

School Mate Publishing

One of the most exciting moments for students may happen when they behold an actual published work of their own creation. School Mate Publishing (www.schoolmatepublishing.com) was created with this in mind.

This site allows students to become published authors and receive an actual copy of the book they wrote. This low-cost self-publishing program allows parents to purchase a book of their child's work, and teachers can receive a free copy of the book for their classroom library.

Self-publishing through a company such as School Mate Publishing allows students to learn about the publishing process while improving their writing, organization, and cooperation skills.

Writing and Reviewing Communities

Having reluctant readers review the written work of other students is a great way to get them to read and write. This review process allows reluctant readers to share their thoughts and ideas as they pass along what they learned to others.

Writing.com

Writing.com is a large, online community for writers of any age and skill level. It provides a platform for storing and displaying student work, and it allows students to provide feedback for each other's work.

Members of Writing.com can create their own online writing portfolio, share their work, enjoy access to a number of writing tools, and even enter the site's many contests.

Goodreads

Goodreads, in addition to being the premier online community for reviewing books, learning about new books, and reading other's reviews of books, has a creative writing section (www.goodreads.com/story) that allows budding writers to publish their work to the site and have others read and review it.

Other writing sites for students that are worth exploring include:

- The National Novel Writing Month (Nano Wrimo) website includes a Young Writer's Program (http://ywp.nanowrimo.org) that offers young authors resources such as pep talks, workbooks, helpful links, and the opportunity to meet other writers.

- Young Writer's Online.net (www.youngwriterson-line.net) is a community forum that encourages collaboration and conversation. Students can post a written work to the site and engage in conversations with other students their own age about the writing process.

- KidPub (www.kidpub.org) is a writing contest that allows young kids to get involved in the process of creating and writing books and stories. It also serves as a forum through which students can read, write, and talk about books.

- The Young Writer's Society (www.youngwriterssociety. com) is similar to the other sites listed here; however, it includes a unique feature that allows kids to post their work and, through the number of "likes" received from other readers, have the opportunity for their work to be spotlighted on the site.

Attaining Fluency

The tools and resources noted in this book are designed to help students extend the enjoyment that reading brings, while also demonstrating educational standards that focus on key skills, such as creativity and information fluency. (See ISTE Standards for Students, Appendix B.) When students learn to locate, read, and analyze books, and then create new works based on what they've read, educators can know that they have reached the ultimate goal—successfully curating the reading lives of their students.

The marriage between reading and technology should be a loving relationship that lasts a lifetime. Learning to read is a skill; for some it happens naturally and easily, while for others it is more difficult. Whatever their natural skill level, it is important that students are introduced to the tools they need to develop a positive attitude toward reading and writing.

Technology can act as a natural motivator for children, especially those who are struggling to read. Let's use it to propel students along the path toward literacy. Let us use technology to help students find books, discuss books, and share their own stories with others. Through this experience, students won't merely move from reluctance to fluency, they will savor the adventure along the way.

Appendix A

Apps to Inspire Even the Most Reluctant Readers

A great learning app for students should entertain them, pique their interest, and spark their curiosity. Students will think they are playing a video game, but parents and educators will know that these games are in fact learning activities designed to challenge and engage young learners. From puzzle apps and book apps to games and creative adventures, there are seemingly endless varieties of children's apps available through both iTunes and Google Play, with new ones popping up every day. Because it can be a frustrating endeavor to navigate the crowded app store in search of something worthwhile, we've listed a few tried-and-true apps (many of them free!) that are sure to make the grade with your reluctant readers.

Pre-Readers

ABC Animals: iTunes, $1.99
Letters correspond to animals, teaches upper and lowercase letters, the pronunciation of letters, and animal names.

ABC Letter Tracing: iTunes, free
Helps pre-readers recognize and write the alphabet using encouraging words and adorable pictures.

abc PocketPhonics: iTunes, $6.99
Early reader tool for listening to the sounds of letters by themselves and when combined with other letters.

Duck Duck Moose Reading: iTunes, Google Play, $1.99
Introduces beginning readers to phonics, spelling, lowercase letters, and sound-out words.

First Words Sampler: iTunes, free
This app gives preschoolers their first look at letters and words using colorful sounds and pictures.

LetterSchool: iTunes, Google Play, free
Teaches pre-readers letter shapes, names, and sounds.

MeeGenius: iTunes, Google Play, free
Engage the littlest readers and pre-readers by personalizing stories and highlighting words for review.

Montessori Crosswords: iTunes, Google Play, $2.99
Teaches letter sounds through mini-crossword puzzles.

Read Me Stories: iTunes, Google Play, free
Provides pre-readers with a new book every day.

Reading Rainbow: iTunes, free
Provides readers with a library of more than 200 books, all narrated by Reading Rainbow's beloved host, LeVar Burton.

Reading Raven HD: iTunes, $3.99
Children can trace letters, decode simple words, and record themselves reading.

Speech with Milo – Sequencing: iTunes, Google Play, $2.99
Sequencing game for pre-readers/early readers that encourages children to put a series of pictures in order.

Storia (Scholastic): www.scholastic.com, free
Creates a virtual bookshelf and organizes all reading content by both age and reading level, making it easy for kids to choose their own books.

A Story Before Bed: iTunes, free
Provides access to more than 300 stories, as well as a unique recording feature that lets you record story time for later viewing.

Super Why! PBS Kids: iTunes, Google Play, $2.99
Four different games to excite the youngest readers and pre-readers.

Tales2Go (Parents' Choice Gold Award recipient):
iTunes, Google Play, free
Streams more than 1,000 stories on-demand, all of which are organized by age, genre, and more.

Early Readers

Grace App for Autism: Google Play, $9.99
Developed by a mother of an autistic child, this app helps with sentence building by providing the images needed to form a sentence.

Me Books: iTunes, Google Play, free
Hear the story aloud and read along; allows readers to record themselves reading along.

Opposite Ocean: iTunes, $.99
Teaches readers antonyms while they earn "pearls" when
they drag the right word to the enchanted clam.

Reading Eggs Sight Words: iTunes, free
Allows children to crack "eggs" by recognizing a sight
word that is the same as the word spoken.

Rock 'N Learn Phonics Easy Reader: iTunes, $1.99
Read phonics stories, tap phonics words for help; younger
readers can have the stories read to them.

Sight Words List: iTunes, free
Helps beginning readers memorize and recall sight words;
all sight words are broken down by age.

Starfall Learn to Read: iTunes, Google Play, $2.99
Provides a plethora of online reading games.

Storia (Scholastic): www.scholastic.com, free
Creates a virtual bookshelf and organizes all reading
content by both age and reading level, thereby making
it easy for kids to choose their own books.

Word Magic: iTunes, $.99
Hones spelling skills by challenging kids to complete the
words with missing letters.

Advanced Readers

Reading Trainer: iTunes, Google Play, $2.99
Helps readers increase their reading speed and ability.

Storia (Scholastic): www.scholastic.com, free
Creates a virtual bookshelf and organizes all reading content by both age and reading level, making it easy for kids to choose their own books.

Word Sort by Grammaropolis: iTunes, $1.99
This is a winner among apps, as it helps kids learn about the parts of speech, like nouns, verbs, and adverbs, while also teaching grammar skills.

Writing Prompts by Writing.com: iTunes, Google Play, $1.99
Provides students with fresh ideas for their writing assignments.

Readers with Disabilities

Dragon Dictation: iTunes, free
A speech-to-text app, it transforms spoken words into written text.

Find the Letters HD: iTunes, $4.99
Challenges users to find letters and numbers within a coloring grid; ideal for helping with skill building in depth orientation, form discrimination, and concentration.

Idea Sketch: iTunes, free
A mind-mapping app for students who need help organizing their ideas so that they can translate ideas into written work.

Prizmo: iTunes, $9.99
Ideal for struggling readers, this app allows users to scan a text document and listen as it is read out loud.

Sound Literacy: iTunes, $24.99
This app for children with dyslexia utilizes the Gillingham method.

Speak It!: Google Play, free
This app by Triple Education provides a text-to-speech option for readers with disabilities to receive the extra help they may need.

Talk to Me: iTunes, $1.99
Another text-to-speech app that allows individuals to listen to how the words sound as they are typed.

Handwriting

Handwriting Without Tears: iTunes, $6.99
Teaches writers the correct format for writing capitals, numbers, and lowercase letters.

iWriteWords: iTunes, $2.99
Focused on handwriting and writing letters and words; encourages with attractive drawings.

Letter Writer Oceans: iTunes, $.99
Visually beautiful pre-reader tool that teaches pre-readers to write the letters of the alphabet.

Writing

Book Creator: Google Play, $2.49
Create everything from magazines to comic books; ideal for writers of all ages.

The Land of Me—Story Time: iTunes, $2.99
Allows children to create their own stories by choosing characters, story lines, and endings.

Storyrobe: iTunes, $.99
Allows writers to share their own stories and share them via YouTube or email.

Comprehension

Question Builder: iTunes, $5.99
Solid readers are encouraged to use their critical thinking, comprehension, and abstract thinking skills.

MiniMod Reading for Details Lite: iTunes, $3.99
Comprehension app helps readers identify the who, what, when, where, and why of reading.

Vocabulary/Grammar/Spelling Skills

Chicktionary—Spelling and Vocabulary:
iTunes, Google Play, free
For grades 2–12, this app hones spelling skills while helping readers stay entertained and encouraged with squawking chickens.

Co:Writer: iTunes, $19.99
A writing app that aids readers and writers with phonetic spelling, grammar, and vocabulary; accesses more than 4 million topic-specific dictionaries.

Duck Duck Moose Reading: iTunes, Google Play, $1.99
Introduces beginning readers to phonics, spelling,
lowercase letters, and sounding out words.

I Spell My Words: iTunes, $3.99
Helps readers and writers of all abilities learn how to spell
words using meaningful images and videos.

Miss Spell's Class: iTunes, Google Play, free
Readers test their spelling skills by guessing which round
of 20 words are spelled correctly or incorrectly.

The Opposites: iTunes, $.99
Helps readers learn words and their antonyms by
matching pairs of opposite words; offers 10 levels for
children of all ages.

Sentence Builder: iTunes, $5.99
Ideal for elementary-aged children learning to build
grammatically correct sentences.

The Spelling Bee: iTunes, $1.99
Provides three levels of spelling games.

Word Magic: iTunes, $.99; Google Play, $1.50
Helps elementary-aged children learn and spell new words
using rewards and other positive reinforcement.

Word Wagon: iTunes, $1.99
Phonics and spelling skills, features more than 100 words,
plus adorable graphics.

Wordle: iTunes, Google Play, $.99
Boggle-type app that is ideal for all levels of spellers.

Appendix B

ISTE Standards

ISTE Standards for Students (ISTE Standards•S)

All K–12 students should be prepared to meet the following standards and performance indicators.

1. Creativity and Innovation

Students demonstrate creative thinking, construct knowledge, and develop innovative products and processes using technology. Students:

   a. apply existing knowledge to generate new ideas, products, or processes

   b. create original works as a means of personal or group expression

   c. use models and simulations to explore complex systems and issues

   d. identify trends and forecast possibilities

2. Communication and Collaboration

Students use digital media and environments to communicate and work collaboratively, including at a distance, to support individual learning and contribute to the learning of others. Students:

a. interact, collaborate, and publish with peers, experts, or others employing a variety of digital environments and media

b. communicate information and ideas effectively to multiple audiences using a variety of media and formats

c. develop cultural understanding and global awareness by engaging with learners of other cultures

d. contribute to project teams to produce original works or solve problems

3. Research and Information Fluency

Students apply digital tools to gather, evaluate, and use information. Students:

a. plan strategies to guide inquiry

b. locate, organize, analyze, evaluate, synthesize, and ethically use information from a variety of sources and media

c. evaluate and select information sources and digital tools based on the appropriateness to specific tasks

d. process data and report results

4. Critical Thinking, Problem Solving, and Decision Making

Students use critical-thinking skills to plan and conduct research, manage projects, solve problems, and make informed decisions using appropriate digital tools and resources. Students:

a. identify and define authentic problems and significant questions for investigation

b. plan and manage activities to develop a solution or complete a project

c. collect and analyze data to identify solutions and make informed decisions

d. use multiple processes and diverse perspectives to explore alternative solutions

5. Digital Citizenship

Students understand human, cultural, and societal issues related to technology and practice legal and ethical behavior. Students:

a. advocate and practice the safe, legal, and responsible use of information and technology

b. exhibit a positive attitude toward using technology that supports collaboration, learning, and productivity

c. demonstrate personal responsibility for lifelong learning

d. exhibit leadership for digital citizenship

6. Technology Operations and Concepts

Students demonstrate a sound understanding of technology concepts, systems, and operations. Students:

a. understand and use technology systems

b. select and use applications effectively and productively

c. troubleshoot systems and applications

d. transfer current knowledge to the learning of new technologies

ISTE Standards for Teachers (ISTE Standards•T)

All classroom teachers should be prepared to meet the following standards and performance indicators.

1. **Facilitate and Inspire Student Learning and Creativity**

   Teachers use their knowledge of subject matter, teaching and learning, and technology to facilitate experiences that advance student learning, creativity, and innovation in both face-to-face and virtual environments. Teachers:

   a. promote, support, and model creative and innovative thinking and inventiveness

   b. engage students in exploring real-world issues and solving authentic problems using digital tools and resources

   c. promote student reflection using collaborative tools to reveal and clarify students' conceptual understanding and thinking, planning, and creative processes

   d. model collaborative knowledge construction by engaging in learning with students, colleagues, and others in face-to-face and virtual environments

2. **Design and Develop Digital-Age Learning Experiences and Assessments**

   Teachers design, develop, and evaluate authentic learning experiences and assessments incorporating contemporary tools and resources to maximize content learning in context and to develop the knowledge, skills, and attitudes identified in the ISTE Standards for Students. Teachers:

a. design or adapt relevant learning experiences that incorporate digital tools and resources to promote student learning and creativity

b. develop technology-enriched learning environments that enable all students to pursue their individual curiosities and become active participants in setting their own educational goals, managing their own learning, and assessing their own progress

c. customize and personalize learning activities to address students' diverse learning styles, working strategies, and abilities using digital tools and resources

d. provide students with multiple and varied formative and summative assessments aligned with content and technology standards and use resulting data to inform learning and teaching

3. Model Digital-Age Work and Learning

Teachers exhibit knowledge, skills, and work processes representative of an innovative professional in a global and digital society. Teachers:

a. demonstrate fluency in technology systems and the transfer of current knowledge to new technologies and situations

b. collaborate with students, peers, parents, and community members using digital tools and resources to support student success and innovation

c. communicate relevant information and ideas effectively to students, parents, and peers using a variety of digital-age media and formats

d. model and facilitate effective use of current and emerging digital tools to locate, analyze, evaluate, and use information resources to support research and learning

4. Promote and Model Digital Citizenship and Responsibility

Teachers understand local and global societal issues and responsibilities in an evolving digital culture and exhibit legal and ethical behavior in their professional practices. Teachers:

a. advocate, model, and teach safe, legal, and ethical use of digital information and technology, including respect for copyright, intellectual property, and the appropriate documentation of sources

b. address the diverse needs of all learners by using learner-centered strategies and providing equitable access to appropriate digital tools and resources

c. promote and model digital etiquette and responsible social interactions related to the use of technology and information

d. develop and model cultural understanding and global awareness by engaging with colleagues and students of other cultures using digital-age communication and collaboration tools

5. Engage in Professional Growth and Leadership

Teachers continuously improve their professional practice, model lifelong learning, and exhibit leadership in their school and professional community by promoting and demonstrating the effective use of digital tools and resources. Teachers:

a. participate in local and global learning communities to explore creative applications of technology to improve student learning

b. exhibit leadership by demonstrating a vision of technology infusion, participating in shared decision making and community building, and developing the leadership and technology skills of others

c. evaluate and reflect on current research and professional practice on a regular basis to make effective use of existing and emerging digital tools and resources in support of student learning

d. contribute to the effectiveness, vitality, and self-renewal of the teaching profession and of their school and community

Index